Your Government:
How It Works

The Federal Bureau of Investigation

Dynise Balcavage

Arthur M. Schlesinger, jr.
Senior Consulting Editor

ouse Publishers
Philadelphia

CHELSEA HOUSE PUBLISHERS

Editor in Chief Stephen Reginald
Production Manager Pamela Loos
Art Director Sara Davis
Director of Photography Judy L. Hasday
Managing Editor James D. Gallagher
Senior Production Editor LeeAnne Gelletly

Staff for THE FEDERAL BUREAU OF INVESTIGATION

Project Editor Anne Hill
Project Editor/Publishing Coordinator Jim McAvoy
Associate Art Director Takeshi Takahashi
Series Designer Takeshi Takahashi, Keith Trego

The Chelsea House World Wide Web address is
http://www.chelseahouse.com

3 5 7 9 8 6 4 2

Library of Congress Cataloging-in-Publication Data

Balcavage, Dynise.
      The Federal Bureau of Investigation / by Dynise Balcavage.
            p. cm. — (Your government—how it works)
      Includes bibliographical references and index.
      Summary: Discusses the history of the FBI, the Federal Bureau
of Investigation, and some of its most famous cases.
      ISBN 0-7910-5530-2 (hc.)
      1. United States. Federal Bureau of Investigation—History—
Juvenile literature. 2. Criminal investigation—United States—
Juvenile literature. [1. United States. Federal Bureau of Investigation. 2. Criminal investigation.] I. Title. II. Series.

HV8144.F43 B35 2000
363.25'0973—dc21   99-048916

Contents

YOUR GOVERNMENT HOW IT WORKS

Introduction

Government: Crises of Confidence

Arthur M. Schlesinger, jr.

FROM THE START, Americans have regarded their government with a mixture of reliance and mistrust. The men who founded the republic understood the importance of government. "If men were angels," observed the 51st Federalist Paper, "no government would be necessary." But men are not angels. Because human beings are subject to wicked as well as to noble impulses, government was deemed essential to assure freedom and order.

The American revolutionaries, however, also knew that government could become a source of injury and oppression. The men who gathered in Philadelphia in 1787 to write the Constitution therefore had two purposes in mind: They wanted to establish a strong central authority and to limit that central authority's capacity to abuse its power.

To prevent the abuse of power, the Founding Fathers wrote two basic principles into the Constitution. The principle of federalism divided power between the state governments and the central authority. The principle of the separation of powers subdivided the central authority itself into three branches—the executive, the legislative, and the judiciary—so that "each may be a check on the other."

YOUR GOVERNMENT: HOW IT WORKS examines some of the major parts of that central authority, the federal government. It explains how various officials, agencies, and departments operate and explores the political organizations that have grown up to serve the needs of government.

Introduction

The federal government as presented in the Constitution was more an idealistic construct than a practical administrative structure. It was barely functional when it came into being.

This was especially true of the executive branch. The Constitution did not describe the executive branch in any detail. After vesting executive power in the president, it assumed the existence of "executive departments" without specifying what these departments should be. Congress began defining their functions in 1789 by creating the Departments of State, Treasury, and War.

President Washington, assisted by Secretary of the Treasury Alexander Hamilton, equipped the infant republic with a working administrative structure. Congress also continued that process by creating more executive departments as they were needed.

Throughout the 19th century, the number of federal government workers increased at a consistently faster rate than did the population. Increasing concerns about the politicization of public service led to efforts—bitterly opposed by politicians—to reform it in the latter part of the century.

The 20th century saw considerable expansion of the federal establishment. More importantly, it saw growing impatience with bureaucracy in society as a whole.

The Great Depression during the 1930s confronted the nation with its greatest crisis since the Civil War. Under Franklin Roosevelt, the New Deal reshaped the federal government, assigning it a variety of new responsibilities and greatly expanding its regulatory functions. By 1940, the number of federal workers passed the 1 million mark.

Critics complained of big government and bureaucracy. Business owners resented federal regulation. Conservatives worried about the impact of paternalistic government on self-reliance, on community responsibility, and on economic and personal freedom.

When the United States entered World War II in 1941, government agencies focused their energies on supporting the war effort. By the end of World War II, federal civilian employment had risen to 3.8 million. With peace, the federal establishment declined to around 2 million in 1950. Then growth resumed, reaching 2.8 million by the 1980s.

A large part of this growth was the result of the national government assuming new functions such as: affirmative action in civil rights, environmental protection, and safety and health in the workplace.

Some critics became convinced that the national government was a steadily growing behemoth swallowing up the liberties of the people. The 1980s brought new intensity to the debate about government growth. Foes of Washington bureaucrats preferred local government, feeling it more responsive to popular needs.

But local government is characteristically the government of the locally powerful. Historically, the locally powerless have often won their human and constitutional rights by appealing to the national government. The national government has defended racial justice against local bigotry, upheld the Bill of Rights against local vigilantism, and protected natural resources from local greed. It has civilized industry and secured the rights of labor organizations. Had the states' rights creed prevailed, perhaps slavery would still exist in the United States.

Americans are still of two minds. When pollsters ask large, spacious questions—Do you think government has become too involved in your lives? Do you think government should stop regulating business?—a sizable majority opposes big government. But when asked specific questions about the practical work of government—Do you favor Social Security? Unemployment compensation? Medicare? Health and safety standards in factories? Environmental protection?—a sizable majority approves of intervention.

We do not like bureaucracy, but we cannot live without it. We need its genius for organizing the intricate details of our daily lives. Without bureaucracy, modern society would collapse. It would be impossible to run any of the large public and private organizations we depend on without bureaucracy's division of labor and hierarchy of authority. The challenge is to keep these necessary structures of our civilization flexible, efficient, and capable of innovation.

More than 200 years after the drafting of the Constitution, Americans still rely on government but also mistrust it. These attitudes continue to serve us well. What we mistrust, we are more likely to monitor. And government needs our constant attention if it is to avoid inefficiency, incompetence, and arbitrariness. Without our informed participation, it cannot serve us individually or help us as a people to attain the lofty goals of the Founding Fathers.

The FBI laboratory, one of the biggest and best equipped forensic laboratories in the world, has been housed in the J. Edgar Hoover building in Washington, D.C., since 1974. The FBI receives so much mail it has its own zip code.

CHAPTER 1

Crime and Punishment:
A Look at a Few of the FBI's Most Famous Cases

The Birth of the FBI's Most Wanted

IN 1949 SAM FOGG, a reporter for the International News Service, was looking for ideas for a story. He called FBI headquarters and asked them for information about the 10 toughest guys they were trying to capture. Fogg gathered the information and wrote stories about these fugitives. The publicity these stories created helped the FBI to capture two of the men on the list.

J. Edgar Hoover, who was then the director of the FBI, realized that the most wanted list was an extremely important crime-fighting tool. In 1950 he decided to come up with a permanent list of the FBI's Ten Most Wanted Fugitives and to send it to newspapers all over the United States. In addition, small stores and post offices hung larger posters showing the criminals' faces and a list of their offenses. The result? From the first Most Wanted list of criminals, nine were caught with the help of these posters and newspaper stories.

To this day, this highly effective list is used to capture criminals. Thanks to technology, the faces and rap sheets of the "members" of this infamous club also grace the FBI's website and often make unknowing "guest appearances" on TV shows such as *America's Most Wanted* and *Unsolved Mysteries*. With the help of the mass media, more people are able to see these criminals, thereby increasing the likelihood that someone will recognize them and turn them in or disclose their whereabouts.

Once a Most Wanted criminal is caught, the FBI replaces him with another fugitive. FBI agents must choose from a list of about 6,000 fugitives. Criminals can only be put on the Most Wanted list if they meet the following requirements:

J. Edgar Hoover, director of the FBI, created the FBI's Ten Most Wanted Fugitives list in 1950.

1. They must be considered a "dangerous menace to society."
2. They must be wanted for a federal crime or they must have crossed state lines in order to avoid being prosecuted in a state.
3. FBI agents must believe that making the criminal's information public will lead to an arrest.
4. The criminal's real identity must be known.
5. The criminals must be interesting enough to create public interest.

A Very Charming Killer

On January 31, 1974, Linda Healy did not show up for work. Later that evening, she missed a dinner engagement. Her friends and family were concerned and called the Seattle, Washington, police. Detectives searched her apartment and found her blood-soaked nightgown and some bloody sheets in her room.

Over the next five months, women throughout the Seattle area continued to disappear, seemingly without a trace. Interestingly, these women all looked alike: they were all young and pretty and had dark, shoulder-length hair, which they wore parted down the middle. They all disappeared in the evening.

A few put up a fight and managed to escape. They described their assailant as either walking with the aid of crutches or as having a broken arm and wearing a cast. The young man would ask the women for help carrying books. The good samaritans who chose to help the man usually ended up dead.

The man in the cast was named Theodore Robert Bundy. A handsome law school dropout, Bundy was active in politics, did volunteer work, and was even applauded by Seattle police for saving the life of a boy who was drowning in a local lake. To strangers, he seemed charming, witty, and intelligent.

Serial killer Theodore Robert Bundy, who eluded local police in the 1970s, was eventually captured and convicted with the help of FBI agents.

Bundy, however, was not the angel he appeared to be. Police eventually caught up with him and arrested him for murder in 1977. He managed to escape from police custody and continued to blaze his trail of horrific crimes.

Bundy beat two sleeping women to death and severely injured two others at a sorority house at Florida State University. In February 1978 he raped and killed a 12-year-old girl named Kimberly Leach. Four days later, officials added Bundy's name to the most wanted list. Florida police caught up with him just five days later when they recognized the stolen license plates on his car.

Serial killer Ted Bundy is just one criminal that FBI agents worked successfully to convict and prosecute. As you will discover, some of the world's most famous crime cases have been solved by (or with the help of) the FBI, one of the world's most famous and well-respected law enforcement agencies.

Terror in the Skies

On December 21, 1988, Pan Am flight 103 exploded and pieces of the plane fell onto the picturesque Scottish town of Lockerbie, killing 259 people on the plane and 11

Alleged Massachusetts mobster James J. "Whitey" Bulger is officially placed on the Ten Most Wanted Fugitives list in August 1999. The list, used by the FBI since 1950, is now displayed on television and the Internet.

people on the ground. Sadly, many people on board were on their way to visit friends and family for the holidays. Officials suspected a terrorist bombing, and they called in the FBI to investigate. Putting together the pieces of this tragic puzzle was no easy task. Because of heavy cross-winds, wreckage fragments were scattered over 845 miles of Scotland.

After much research, FBI officials determined that a bomb did, in fact, cause the plane to explode. Among other clues investigators found fragments having jagged edges and coated with soot—certain evidence that an explosion had taken place.

The FBI's painstaking investigation into the explosion of Pan Am flight 103 over Lockerbie, Scotland, led to the identification and arrest of the Libyan terrorists responsible for the bombing.

Among the millions of other fragments, investigators also discovered a small piece of circuit board. They learned that it was made for European radios; and after more research, they determined that it came from a Toshiba radio. Almost a year after the crash, a scientist found another tiny piece of circuit board embedded in clothing from a suitcase. It was a circuit board different from that of the Toshiba. As it turned out, the manufacturer of this specific board confirmed that they had recently delivered a supply of 20 of these circuit boards to the North African nation of Libya. The FBI determined that the bomb was hidden in a cassette player within a suitcase.

Investigators also traced clothing fragments back to Libya. They determined that one of the suspects hid a bomb in a Toshiba radio cassette player, which he then hid within a suitcase. Because this suspect was an employee of Libyan Arab Airlines on the island of Malta, he did not have to go through the usual security measures. Without being detected, he planted the suitcase on an Air Malta plane flying to Frankfurt, Germany. Because the bomb was designed to blow up at a high altitude, it did not explode at the lower altitude at which the Air Malta plane flew. In Frankfurt, unknowing employees loaded the suitcase on to a 727 airplane flying to London. At London's Heathrow Airport it was finally transferred to the New York-bound Pan Am 747, which made that fatal flight to Lockerbie. Half an hour after takeoff, at a height of 31,000 feet, Pan Am flight 103 exploded over the Scottish town.

Investigators then painstakingly determined how much explosive material was used and where exactly the bomb had been placed in the container.

They concluded that it was indeed a terrorist attack that took the lives of so many innocent people, and so they set out to identify the culprits and to prosecute them.

Thanks to the help of FBI experts and various law enforcement officials, the suspects were apprehended and were extradited to Scotland to face charges. Abdel Basset and Lamen Khalifa Ffimah were indicted in November 1991 and are currently undergoing trial in Scotland.

CHAPTER **2**

The Birth of the FBI: A Brief History

THE ORGANIZATION WE KNOW as the FBI came about by way of a group of special agents that Attorney General Charles Bonaparte formed in 1908, when Theodore Roosevelt was president of the United States.

Bonaparte and Roosevelt first got to know each other in 1892—early in their respective careers—at a meeting of the Baltimore Civil Service Reform Association. Roosevelt, who at the time was the civil service commissioner, bragged about the improvements he had brought about in federal law enforcement.

The Progressive Era

In the late 1800s, most people entered into government jobs as a result of their connections to important people in politics. Neither Roosevelt nor Bonaparte approved of this practice; they thought it was unfair and that it encouraged mediocrity. The two men believed

people holding government positions should be well qualified and should possess a good deal of expertise in their
fields. For their beliefs, Roosevelt and Bonaparte were la-
beled progressives.

In 1901, Vice President Roosevelt became president of
the United States after the assassination of President
McKinley. Roosevelt was elected into the office in 1904.
In 1906, in keeping with his progressive beliefs, he named
Bonaparte as his attorney general, the chief law officer and
legal counsel of the United States of America. Roosevelt
had a great deal of faith in Bonaparte's abilities and wanted
to put them to use. Two years later Bonaparte founded a
group of highly qualified, capable special agents within
the Department of Justice, the branch of government that
oversees the legal system. Although this corps had neither
a name nor an official leader other than Bonaparte, these
special agents were the foundation of what is now known
as the Federal Bureau of Investigation.

At the time, citizens were not altogether convinced that
the development of a service that would investigate federal (national) crimes would work. The United States Constitution is based on the concept of federalism. Through
this concept the federal government could preside over issues that crossed states' boundaries, as in the example of a
highway being built across several states. All other government powers, including the investigation of criminal
acts, however, were reserved for the states. People were
used to the government operating in this manner.

Because of better and faster means of transportation
and more accessible forms of communication, such as the
radio and the telephone, people's opinions about who
should control criminal investigations changed. By the turn
of the century, people became more comfortable with the
idea of the federal government ruling over certain issues.
Most people felt that, with the government's help, they
could prosper and grow. They believed that only by hiring
experts in various areas of industry, could the United States

continue to develop. Thus the period from 1900 to 1918 became known as the Progressive Era.

During this time the Department of Justice under Bonaparte had no investigators of its own except for a few special agents who carried out specific assignments for the attorney general and a few examiners (trained as accountants) who reviewed the financial transactions of the federal courts.

By 1907 the Department of Justice used Secret Service men to conduct investigations. These men were well trained and capable, but they reported to the chief of the Secret Service and not to the attorney general. This frustrated Bonaparte; he wanted complete control over investigations. On May 27, 1908, Congress passed a law preventing the Department of Justice from engaging Secret Service operatives.

The next month Bonaparte appointed a force of special agents within the Department of Justice. The force included 10 former Secret Service employees and a number of Department of Justice workers. They became special agents of the Department of Justice. On July 26, 1908, Bonaparte ordered them to report to Chief Examiner Stanley W. Finch. This order is considered the official beginning of the FBI.

Both Attorney General Bonaparte and President Theodore Roosevelt, who finished their terms in March 1909, recommended that the force of 34 agents become a permanent part of the Department of Justice. Attorney General George Wickersham, Bonaparte's successor, named the crew of investigators the Bureau of Investigation on March 16, 1909. At that time the title of chief examiner was changed to chief of the Bureau of Investigation.

Growing Pains

During the FBI's formative years, the bureau investigated violations of some of the few existing federal laws, such as bankruptcy frauds, antitrust crime, and neutrality violations. During World War I, the bureau was given responsibility for investigating espionage, **sabotage,** sedition, draft violations, and eventually, motor vehicle thefts.

Table 2-1   A Timeline of the FBI's Various Names

Date	FBI's Various Names
July 26, 1908	No specific name assigned; referred to as Special Agent Force
March 16, 1909	Bureau of Investigation
July 1, 1932	United States Bureau of Investigation
August 10, 1933	Division of Investigation (The division also included the Bureau of Prohibition.)
July 1, 1935	Federal Bureau of Investigation

Almost immediately, the new agency had publicity problems. When the United States entered World War I, the Bureau of Investigation rounded up thousands of young men whom they believed to be draft dodgers. (When a man turns 18, he must register with the U.S. Civil Service for the draft. The government maintains a pool of young men whom it can enlist, or draft, into the Armed Services in case America goes to war.) In truth, only a few men dodged the draft.

Not long after the war, the bureau led the Palmer Raids in which tens of thousands of alien (people from other countries) radicals were arrested in 33 American cities. In the United States, however, you must have a warrant to arrest someone. Because the agents had few warrants, most of these men were eventually released

A law called Prohibition passed in 1920. This law made it illegal to make, sell, or consume alcohol. With the passing of this strict rule, the gangster era was born. The years from 1921 to 1933 are often called the "lawless years," because of all the gangster activity and because of the public's disregard for Prohibition. In 1934, many new federal criminal statutes were passed, and Congress decided to allow special agents to carry firearms.

J. Edgar Hoover

One of the leaders of the Palmer Raids was a young lawyer named J. Edgar Hoover. In 1924 Hoover was cho-

An illegal brewing operation is broken up by federal agents in the early days of Prohibition. The guns the agents are holding were confiscated along with the liquor barrels and brewing bottles.

sen to reorganize the stuggling agency. In 1935 it was re-named the Federal Bureau of Investigation. Hoover served as the FBI's director until his death in 1972. Hoover cleaned up the disorganized agency and gained fame for tracking down, with the help of his special agents, crimi-nals like John Dillinger, Pretty Boy Floyd, and Baby Face Nelson.

Hoover, however, overstepped his bounds many times during his career. Even though the FBI's primary function was to look into violations of federal law, Hoover and his agents, or G-men, a nickname for government men, even-tually investigated offenses such as shipping stolen goods and obscenity in literature.

After World War II, a period known as the Cold War began between the Soviet Union and the United States. Generally speaking, Americans feared communists, partic-ularly Soviet communists. (Communism is a system of government in which a single party holds power. This party maintains order in the country, and all people share in the ownership of all goods.) Americans were afraid that the world's other superpower, the Union of Soviet Socialist Republics (USSR), would begin a nuclear war.

Senator Joseph McCarthy's 1951–1954 hearings on communist activity in Hollywood led to the creation of a blacklist of writers and performers believed to be communist collaborators.

In 1947 the House Un-American Activities Committee investigated people they suspected of being communists. Hoover singled out artists, writers, and performers whom he and his cronies considered as having left wing, or liberal, beliefs. He suspected these individuals of collaborating with the communists. Unfortunately, the investigations often had little basis. Although his intentions might have been good, he ruined the careers and indeed the lives of many of these people without any regard to their free speech rights.

Later in the 1960s, Hoover began to distrust people involved in the civil rights movement—the movement in which people fought against discrimination on the basis of race. He even spied on black leaders and tried to destroy their cause and also tried to undermine the women's liberation movement when it started in the late 1960s and early 1970s. This information was classified, and members of the FBI hid it from the public.

Despite his foibles, Hoover is largely remembered as an effective leader who transformed the FBI from a bumbling, disorganized agency into one of the world's most respected law enforcement bureaus.

The FBI Seal

The FBI adopted its colorful seal in 1940. Practically every design element symbolizes either virtues the FBI represents or American historical data.

The blue background and the scales decorating the shield stand for justice. The circle of 13 stars represents the 13 original states and the idea of unity. The laurel leaf symbolizes academic honors, distinction, and fame. The two branches contain 46 leaves, representing the 46 states in the America of 1908, the year the FBI was founded. The red parallel stripes represent courage, valor, and strength; and the white stripes symbolize cleanliness, light, truth, and peace. Just as on the American flag, there is one more red bar than white bar.

The FBI's motto, "Fidelity, Bravery, Integrity," is written on the white banner. The raised edge around the seal stands for the challenges the FBI must face. The seal contains a lot of gold, and this represents its overall value.

The Freedom of Information Act

The Freedom of Information Act was passed in 1966. Because this law did not apply to law enforcement files, FBI files were legally hidden from the public eye.

In 1975, however, the Freedom of Information Act was amended and the Privacy Act of 1974 went into effect. Papers that had previously been off limits to the public were now available to anyone who was willing to complete the paperwork. Many people chose to exercise their new right.

All of these new requests put a tremendous new burden on the FBI. They had to develop an organized, efficient system that would be able to handle the numerous requests for information. They also had to hire the people to maintain these systems.

In the past two decades, the FBI has processed more than 300,000 requests for information. More than six million pages of FBI documents have been released to the

Table 2-2 Leaders of the Federal Bureau of Investigation and Predecessor Agencies

Leader	Date Assumed Office
Stanley W. Finch	July 26, 1908
Alexander Bruce Bielaski	April 30, 1912
William E. Allen (acting)	February 10, 1919
William J. Flynn	July 1, 1919
William J. Burns	August 22, 1921
J. Edgar Hoover	May 10, 1924 (acting)
	December 10, 1924 (permanent)
L. Patrick Gray (acting)	May 3, 1972
William D. Ruckelshaus (acting)	April 27, 1973
Clarence M. Kelley	July 9, 1973
William H. Webster	February 23, 1978
John E. Otto (acting)	May 26, 1987
William S. Sessions	November 2, 1987
Floyd I. Clarke (acting)	July 19, 1993
Louis J. Freeh	September 1, 1993

public. That's a lot of paper, so now the FBI is working on putting the appropriate files online.

Today's FBI

Louis J. Freeh was sworn in as director of the FBI on September 1, 1993. When he made his first speech, he stated his goals: greater cooperation between the FBI and other law enforcement agencies, both at home and overseas, and a restructuring of the organization to make sure it was operating as efficiently as possible.

Freeh quickly achieved these goals. He also wanted to tighten the FBI's standards of conduct, reasoning that FBI employees must be held up as role models. In addition Freeh wanted the bureau's workers to more accurately reflect the nation's diverse population, so in October 1993

he appointed the first woman, the first Hispanic man, and the second African-American man to be named assistant directors. To ensure that the bureau was at the forefront of new technology, Freeh constructed a new FBI forensic laboratory and upgraded the bureau's **surveillance** equipment.

Freeh and the FBI are still working to maintain the FBI's reputation as the world's premier law enforcement agency. They are still carrying out essentially the same mission of that first small group of special agents as well as the tradition of service that has become the bureau's motto: fidelity, bravery, and integrity.

FBI Director Louis J. Freeh talks to the press about investigations of war crimes in Kosovo. One of his goals is greater cooperation between the FBI and overseas law enforcement agencies.

Drug-trafficking is one of the FBI's areas of responsibility. The results of a two-day FBI investigation are strikingly displayed at a 1998 news conference—$1 million in cash and 1,600 pounds of an illegal drug.

CHAPTER **3**

The FBI and Its Responsibilities

THE FBI IS ONE of the world's most respected law enforcement agencies. As the primary investigative arm of the federal government—a sort of police station for government offenses—the FBI enforces over 260 federal statutes (laws) and conducts sensitive national security investigations. Countries all over the globe model their national law enforcement bureaus after the FBI.

According to the FBI's mission statement, the bureau promises "to uphold the law through the investigation of violations of federal criminal law; to protect the United States from foreign **intelligence** and terrorist activities; to provide leadership and law enforcement assistance to federal, state, local, and international agencies; and to perform these responsibilities in a manner that is responsive to the needs of the public and is faithful to the Constitution of the United States."

FBI activities include investigations into organized crime, white-collar crime, public corruption, financial crime, fraud against the government, bribery, copyright matters, civil rights violations, bank robbery, extortion, kidnapping, air piracy, **terrorism,** foreign **counterintelligence,** interstate criminal activity, fugitive and drug-trafficking matters, and other violations of federal statutes.

The FBI also works with other federal, state, and local law enforcement agencies in investigating matters of joint interest and in training law enforcement officers at the FBI Academy.

Division of Labor

Because the FBI is responsible for upholding so many different laws in so many different areas, the bureau is divided into many different departments. Each department concentrates on a different type of crime. This division of labor enables the FBI to run smoothly and efficiently.

Is New York home to more spies than Houston, Texas? Do criminals embezzle more money from banks in Miami, Florida, than in Wilmington, Delaware? Based in Washington, D.C., the FBI has field offices and satellite offices located all over the United States and its territories. The FBI also has offices in several foreign countries. Different areas of the country are allocated various amounts of FBI special agents, according to their needs. After graduating from the FBI Academy, a new special agent is assigned to an FBI field office. Which office a new agent is assigned to depends on the agent's particular area of expertise as well as on the needs of the FBI. As part of their duties, special agents are required to relocate during their careers. They often move several times while they are working for the FBI.

The attorney general of the United States creates guidelines governing the crimes that the FBI investigates. All FBI agents are required to follow the attorney general's guidelines. FBI investigations are divided into several different programs, including civil rights, domestic and international terrorism, foreign counterintelligence, organized crime/drugs, violent crimes and major offenders, and white-collar crimes.

Examples of Investigative Programs
Background Investigations

Anyone who applies to the Department of Energy, the Nuclear Regulatory Commission, the Department of Justice, or the FBI for a job must undergo a background investigation with the FBI's applicant program. This division also conducts background checks for presidential appointees and U.S. court candidates. These investigations involve interviewing neighbors and coworkers of applicants and checking criminal and credit records.

Chief Justice of the United States William Rehnquist, like all United States Supreme Court candidates, underwent an FBI background investigation before taking office.

Civil Rights

First and foremost, the Civil Rights Act of 1964 prohibits discrimination in the workplace. The program also oversees police brutality and housing discrimination matters. The FBI's civil rights program investigates violations of this law and other relevant laws.

Domestic Terrorism

Terrorism is the use of violence and intimidation to achieve a goal or send a message, as occurred in the case of the Pan Am flight 103 bombing that occurred over Lockerbie, Scotland. The FBI leads the fight against terrorism in the United States. The domestic terrorism program looks into threats involving atomic energy, weapons of mass destruction, sabotage (purposely destroying property to stop a cause or endeavor), hostage taking, and civil unrest.

The Lincoln, Montana, cabin of suspected Unabomber Theodore Kaczynski is cordoned off by FBI agents in April 1996. Kaczynski was accused of domestic terrorism for sending bombs through the mail.

National Foreign Intelligence

The FBI is also the lead counterintelligence agency within the U.S. intelligence community. The national foreign intelligence program tries to prevent foreign spies

from obtaining secret information and investigates counterintelligence cases involving people from other countries within U.S. borders. The program also works to investigate other areas, including international terrorism threats and weapons of mass destruction threats.

Al Capone (left, in white hat), shown leaving a Chicago court building, was a well-known organized crime boss of the 1920s.

Organized Crime and Drugs

Many organized crime groups make a great deal of money in drug trafficking (selling drugs for profit). The organized crime drug program investigates these matters and coordinates national organized crime/drug enforcement task forces.

Violent Crimes

The violent crimes and major offenders program (VCMOP) looks into cases in which someone is threatened, injured, or even killed. The cases also include kidnapping, sexual exploitation of children, extortion, bank robbery, consumer product tampering (manipulating products in a store), crimes on Indian reservations, and unlawful flight to avoid prosecution. The VCMOP is also in charge of cases involving threatened or actual assault, kidnapping, or murder involving the president, vice president, or members of Congress.

White-Collar Crimes

The white-collar crime program, the largest of the FBI's criminal programs, targets such criminal activity as money laundering (concealing the source of money, as in drug trafficking), bank fraud (deceiving a bank to obtain money), embezzlement (stealing money, perhaps from an employer), environmental crimes, fraud against the government, health-care fraud, election law violations, and telemarketing fraud.

Child Abduction

When a child disappears, FBI agents interview all of the child's neighbors in order to obtain as much information as possible. They will talk to the child's family and friends to learn what the child is like, what he or she likes to do, and where the child likes to go. Knowing about the child's habits helps the FBI and police determine where they might have gone. Once they eliminate all other possibilities, the police and the FBI may decide that the child has been abducted.

At this point, the FBI's evidence response team might conduct a forensic investigation of the abduction site. They would collect evidence from the spot from which they think the child might have been taken. Scientists would then examine these clues in a lab.

Making the community aware of the situation is extremely important, so anyone who has information about the crime can call the police or the FBI and help in the investigation. An FBI rapid start team, a large computer operation system, organizes and follows tips it receives about the missing child.

FBI special agents and the police also work with the National Center for Missing and Exploited Children and other agencies to make sure they have all the information they need to do their jobs. The more help they receive, the better the chances are of finding the child.

When a law enforcement agency requests information about a missing child, the FBI can give the agency advice about conducting the investigation; create a personality profile of offenders; help publicize a case, perhaps by airing it on television or in the newspapers; and enlist FBI resources such as aircraft surveillance and laboratory assistance.

Cases of assault on the president, such as the attempted assassination of President Ronald Reagan in 1981 (shown here), are investigated by the violent crimes and major offenders program (VCMOP).

Working Together to Fight Crime

The FBI often shares information and collaborates with other federal, state, local, and international law enforcement and intelligence agencies. The FBI is made up of thousands of dedicated law enforcement professionals who work together to achieve the bureau's mission. Highly trained special agents enforce the federal statutes.

Scientists, computer specialists, and other specialty personnel at the Forensic Laboratory, Engineering Research Facility, and the Criminal Justice Information Services Division provide expert assistance in researching and developing cases. Other professionals, in turn, assist these people and help run the day-to-day operations.

Each year the FBI must write a report on its budget and its activities and present it to Congress. During 1996, for example, FBI investigations resulted in 11,855 convictions in federal court. Most of these involved drugs. The next largest chunk involved persons convicted of fraud and bank embezzlement, often through the misuse of credit cards. The third largest grouping was for bank robbery. Overall then, somewhat more than half of all FBI convictions involved drug dealing, scams against financial institutions, and bank robbery.

The bureau is also the lead agency in the investigation of suspected spies and terrorists, an activity that requires considerable resources but rarely results in a prosecution. Another time-consuming FBI responsibility is the investigation of presidential appointees.

The Structure of the FBI

The president appoints the director of the FBI. The Senate confirms the appointee for a term not to exceed 10 years. The present director, Louis J. Freeh, assumed office on September 1, 1993.

Each FBI field office is normally overseen by a special agent in charge (SAC). He or she is helped by at least one assistant special agent in charge (ASAC) as well as by supervisory special agents who manage squads of special agents. Field offices also have an office services manager, who makes sure the office runs smoothly. Because the field offices in New York City and Washington, D.C., are very large, each is managed by an assistant director in charge (ADIC), who is supported by multiple SACs, ASACs, and others.

A resident agent, or a supervisory resident agent, who reports to the SAC overseeing his or her territory, manages each of the 400 field offices. The ADICs manage resident agencies and the SACs are responsible to the director of the FBI, the deputy director, or the assistant directors.

Each legal attaché is headed by one or more assistant legal attachés. They report directly to the Criminal Investigative Division. Each field facility is managed by a special agent and professional support personnel who report to various divisions at FBI headquarters.

CHAPTER **4**

So You Want to Be an FBI Agent?

OFTEN INSPIRED BY ACTION films and television shows, many children dream of someday becoming an FBI agent. But the reality of this demanding job is not as glamorous as these portrayals might suggest.

Becoming a member of the FBI takes hard work, persistence, and dedication. FBI recruits undergo months of extensive, challenging training before they earn the title of special agent. The bureau also has certain qualifications the applicants must meet. Instructors spend a great deal of time making sure the recruits they choose are right for this demanding job. Each year the FBI receives about 10,000 applications from people who want to become special agents, but only about 400 are chosen as recruits in the selection process.

Requirements

In order to become an FBI agent, you must:

1. Be a United States citizen.
2. Be between the ages of 23 and 36 when starting duty.
3. Hold a four-year bachelor's degree from an approved college or university.
4. Have three years of full-time work experience (although law school graduates and graduates with a degree in accounting or with fluency in a foreign language for which the bureau has a need, may not need this three years.
5. Be completely available for assignment anywhere the FBI has offices or needs.
6. Have uncorrected vision (without eyeglasses or prescription lenses) not worse than 20/200 and corrected (with contact lenses or prescription lenses) 20/20 in one eye and not worse than 20/40 in the other eye.
7. Pass a color vision test and possess a valid driver's license.

Because many aspects of the job are unusual, becoming an FBI special agent is not for everyone. Special agents, for example, must be armed or have immediate access to a firearm at all times, even when they are not on official duty. In addition, special agents may be required to utilize deadly force should their lives or the lives of others be in immediate danger.

The Four Programs

When a recruit is accepted into the FBI Academy, located in Quantico, Virginia, he or she must choose an area of specialization, much like students choose a major when they go to college. The FBI Academy has four entry pro-

grams, or majors: law, accounting, language, and diversified. Each has its own educational requirements. Because
the FBI wants its recruits to be mature, well-rounded individuals, its requirements include a combination of educational and work experience.

Law: To qualify under the law program, recruits must
have a **JD** degree from a resident law school.

Accounting: To qualify under the accounting program,
recruits must have earned a BS degree with a major in
accounting or a related discipline and be eligible to
take the certified public accountant (CPA) examination. Candidates who have not passed the CPA exam
must pass the FBI's accounting test.

Language: To qualify under the language program, recruits must have a BS or BA degree in any discipline
and be able to speak fluently a language that meets the
needs of the FBI. Candidates need to pass a language
proficiency test.

Diversified: To qualify under the diversified program,
a recruit must have a BS or BA degree in any discipline plus three years of full-time work experience or
an advanced degree and two years of full-time work
experience.

Even those who want to work for the FBI but do not
want to become special agents must pass a rigid list of requirements. All applicants must be U.S. citizens. Most positions include a test of some sort (either a written or oral
examination), an interview with three special agents, a
physical examination for certain positions, and a drug-
screening test. All applicants must undergo a polygraph,
or lie detector test.

To ensure that the people the bureau hires are compe-
tent and healthy enough to undergo the rigorous work at

the FBI, people at the bureau complete a thorough background investigation on all applicants. Depending on the person and the position, this takes anywhere from one to four months. The bureau contacts former and current employers, references, social acquaintances, and neighbors and asks them questions about the applicant. They might want to know, for example, if the person is dependable, trustworthy, and honest. The applicant's school, credit, arrest, medical, and military records are also reviewed. Officials at the bureau then assess the applicant's complete background information and make a final decision based on what they have learned, whether or not to offer the applicant a job. If, for example, they discover that an applicant has a history of not paying his bills or has received too many traffic violation tickets, the bureau will probably reject the applicant.

The FBI Academy: A Day in the Life of a Rookie

All newly appointed special agents must complete 16 weeks of intensive training at the FBI Academy. The trainees, or **rookies,** spend long days learning the finer points of becoming a special agent. Classes usually start at 7:00 A.M. and go on for about 12 hours.

Rookies study many different subjects in the classroom. Their courses cover organized crime, narcotics, and computer fraud, among other topics. Some of their classwork teaches them to develop skills in investigative techniques, interviewing and interrogating (questioning) suspects, and gathering intelligence information (obtaining secret information). They must learn the details of the approximately 270 laws that the FBI upholds.

Additionally, the trainees undergo intense physical fitness training. They work out in the gym and on the track, learn self-defense techniques, and receive instruction on how to operate firearms. This training is necessary because

An FBI Academy student practices his investigative techniques at a simulated crime scene.

special agents need to be fit enough to survive every imaginable situation. When rookies get tired from the intense workouts, their instructors have little pity. They remind the trainees that running the extra mile might save their lives someday when they are special agents.

The physical and mental tests never stop. Even after rookies have an especially exhausting day, filled with courses, strenuous workouts, and tests, their instructors might challenge them to solve sets of even more complex problems. Although this might sound excessive to nonrecruits, instructors know that these exercises are for the recruits' own good. They want the rookies to be able to think on their feet, even when the recruits feel they are too exhausted to move. Recruits learn to surpass their capabilities and overcome their limitations.

Hogan's Alley

Special agents undergoing FBI Academy training learn methods of investigating areas where crimes were allegedly committed, such as this New Mexico residence.

Every few days the rookies spend time at the FBI Practical Applications Training Unit. Here, in a make-believe town called Hogan's Alley, recruits prepare for real-world situations they might encounter during their careers as FBI agents. This imaginary town includes typical buildings and businesses that exist in most cities: a bank, a drugstore, a courthouse, a used-car lot, a movie theater, a post office, and so on. The idea is to allow rookies to react to dangerous situations they might encounter during their careers as special agents, but within this safe environment.

Instructors create a variety of scenarios to which the rookies must respond. The bank, for example, might be "held up" or a "drug deal" could take place in the used-car lot. A spy could be living in an apartment around the corner. The FBI hires professional actors to play the "bad guys" (after they, too, undergo extensive background checks). Seasoned special agents sometimes play the main parts.

As an added challenge, the instructors encourage the actors to make the situations as difficult as possible for the rookies, so that they will gain experience in dealing with difficult people. If a recruit is "arresting" the bank robber, for example, the actor will not give up without a dramatic, persuasive struggle. All participants stick to the scenario that the instructors create. They even follow a script.

During these play-acting sessions, rookies learn first-hand how to investigate a crime scene, react to a stressful situation, follow FBI rules, and make sure that what they are doing complies with the law. Recruits even go to court in the Hogan's Alley courthouse. Sometimes, the "judge" will throw a case out of court because a rookie has forgotten to follow the proper FBI procedure.

Although these make-believe situations cannot possibly prepare rookies for every situation they will encounter in their careers, they do cover most. When a rookie makes a grave mistake at Hogan's Alley, he is less likely to make the same mistake on the job. When a rookie "shoots" the wrong person at Hogan's Alley, all she will get is a scolding from her instructor. In real life, however, special agents do not get a second chance.

When Lives Are at Risk

Rookies spend long hours in the classroom learning about firearms and put in lots of time on the firing range at Hogan's Alley, sharpening their shooting skills. They learn about different types of weapons and how to operate them. Rookies are taught to use weapons only when lives are at risk.

If a trainee wants extra practice, he can use the firearms automated training system (FATS). This device is similar to a video or computer game. To "play," the trainee stands before a screen. A computer then shows different scenes,

Firing range at the FBI Academy in Quantico, Virginia.

including kidnappings, hold-ups, or hostage scenarios, to which the player must respond. In a matter of seconds, the rookie has to choose whether or not to fire, depending on the situation. If he makes a mistake and fires too late or if he accidentally shoots an innocent person, the game freezes and the words "poor judgment" show up on the screen. This "game" is not really a game at all—the training and decision-making ability it teaches rookies might one day save their lives or the lives of innocent people.

While the training exercises used at Hogan's Alley and in FATS might sound like fun and games, they hold serious consequences for the rookies. Instructors watch the recruits' every move. If a rookie makes too many errors during these exercises, his or her instructor might recommend that the rookie be removed from the training program. Sometimes a trainee will decide, after undergoing the rigorous training, that a career in the FBI is not for him or her.

The Code of Honor

Instructors continually remind FBI rookies of their responsibility. Rookies learn that they must support and defend their partners and the FBI. After enduring all of the training and rigors, they should consider themselves elite and talented, part of the most respected law enforcement agency in the world. They are also reminded that they have a responsibility to U.S. citizens because the agents' salaries are paid through taxes. Lastly, it is enforced that they must always serve and honor the FBI.

Even after the rookies earn their diplomas and the coveted title of special agent which they worked so hard for, the real challenges of their jobs have only just begun. Unlike the actors playing criminals on Hogan's Alley or the video bad guys in the FATS game, the decisions they will face in the real world have actual lives at stake and will affect many people, including themselves.

CHAPTER **5**

Tools of the Trade:
Crime Detection
Tricks the FBI Uses

FBI SPECIAL AGENTS USE a variety of techniques to help them
track down criminals, missing persons, and terrorists. While they are
studying at Quantico, they practice using these techniques. Because
there is a lot to learn, agents might concentrate on a specific area of
investigation and become specialists in one subject. All agents, however, must have a better-than-average comprehension of all available
crime-solving techniques.

Searching for Clues: Ted Bundy

The old myth of a law enforcement official investigating the scene
of a crime with a magnifying glass is not as corny as it might appear.
FBI agents need to find and analyze evidence that may be too tiny for
the naked eye to see. When FBI agents arrive at the scene of a crime,
they will search for fragments, fibers, hairs, paint, footprints, and
trash—all things we ordinarily do not even glance at.

Investigators found tiny fibers from Ted Bundy's coat and the carpet of his van on Kimberly Leach's clothing. These miniscule pieces of evidence, which could have easily been missed, helped convince the jury to convict Ted Bundy for Kimberly Leach's murder, in addition to finding him guilty of several other murders. In 1989 Bundy was put to death in Florida's electric chair.

Creating a Psychological Profile

Investigators can learn a great deal about the criminal by carefully examining the crime scene and the criminal's established behavior patterns. If the crime was excessively violent, for example, the criminal probably knew the victim. If the criminal left the scene tidy, then the criminal is probably a neat person by nature. Investigators can also make educated guesses regarding the criminal's:

- Approximate age, sex, and race
- Upbringing
- Marital status
- Level of education
- Personality traits
- Lifestyle and habits
- Friends or preference for solitude
- Prior criminal record
- Motive for committing a crime
- Next step

The assumptions collected by this process form a psychological profile. This technique was made famous in the movie *The Silence of the Lambs,* in which FBI agents seek a profile of a serial killer.

The FBI created a psychological profile in order to capture the Unabomber—a man who sent deadly mail bombs to several university professors and business-people. (The name is short for university and airline bomber.) His deadly letters killed three people and injured 23 others.

By studying the evidence at the scenes of the crimes, FBI profilers determined that the person was a loner, grew up in the Chicago area, had some connection to Salt Lake City and San Francisco, was intelligent, and was a white male in his fifties.

The FBI's profile was amazingly accurate. As it turned out, the Unabomber, Theodore Kaczynski, lived in a cabin far away from any town or neighbors. He grew up in the Chicago area, worked for a time in Salt Lake City, and taught in the San Francisco area. He had a doctoral degree in mathematics and was a 53-year-old white male.

In April 1996, Kaczynski was arrested. On June 18, 1996, he was charged with four bombings that killed two individuals and injured two others. On October 1, 1996, he was charged with a bombing that killed one individual. At his trial, Kaczynski pled guilty to all of the charged acts as well as bombings for which he was not formally charged. He was sentenced on May 15, 1998, to life in prison with no chance for parole.

The FBI's psychological profile of the Unabomber closely matched the actual facts about Theodore Kaczynski (center), who later confessed to the bombings.

A Case of Mistaken Identity

Before scientists used fingerprint identification to identify criminals, they used a system called the Bertillon system. This technique measured the dimensions of certain skeletal body parts.

In 1903 a man named Will West was booked as a prisoner in the Leavenworth Federal Penitentiary. Besides the fact that West looked a lot like another Leavenworth prisoner, who was coincidentally named William West, prison officials were surprised to find that Will West also had virtually the same Bertillon measurements as his "twin," who was serving a life sentence for murder. Their fingerprints were, of course, different. Realizing that if it were not for **fingerprinting,** the wrong man could have easily been arrested for murder, officials decided to adopt fingerprinting as the standard method of identifying people.

Making Your Mark:
Fingerprinting Identification

Every human being has a unique set of ridges and swirls on his or her fingers. No two are alike. When we touch an object, the sweat and oils on our fingers leave a faint imprint of this pattern, in much the same way as a rubber stamp makes a mark. Ever since the early 1900s, crime fighters have been using fingerprinting to identify and help capture criminals.

When criminals are taken into custody, the officers use ink to make a record of their fingerprints. After collecting over 800,000 fingerprints, most of them from Leavenworth Penitentiary, the FBI started its Identification Division in 1924. This collection was an important crime control tool. Because criminals commonly crossed state lines, having their fingerprints on record made them easier to capture.

Today the FBI holds more than 250 million sets of fingerprint records, made up of both criminal and civil prints.

<table>
<tr><td colspan="2">

Record of
William West
Register No. 2626
</td></tr>
<tr><td>Sentenced</td><td>9-6-1901</td></tr>
<tr><td>Sentence</td><td>Natural Life</td></tr>
<tr><td>Charge</td><td>Murder</td></tr>
<tr><td>Court</td><td>CD-Indian Territory, Case #3692 (South McAlester, Okla)</td></tr>
<tr><td>Received</td><td>9-7-1901</td></tr>
<tr><td>Escaped</td><td>10-22-1916, as trusty from Outside Lawn Detail</td></tr>
<tr><td>Apprehended</td><td>Topeka, Kas. 10-23-1916</td></tr>
<tr><td>Returned</td><td>10-24-1916</td></tr>
<tr><td>Paroled</td><td>8-30-1919</td></tr>
<tr><td>Pardoned</td><td>2-21-1927 (full and unconditional pardon)</td></tr>
<tr><td>Born</td><td>Texas</td></tr>
<tr><td>Left home</td><td>Age 13</td></tr>
<tr><td>Education</td><td>Cannot read nor write</td></tr>
<tr><td>Occupation</td><td>Miner</td></tr>
<tr><td>Religion</td><td>Baptist</td></tr>
<tr><td>Usual Residence</td><td>Tuskahoma, I. T. (Okla)</td></tr>
<tr><td>Father Born</td><td>Place unknown</td></tr>
<tr><td>Mother Born</td><td>Texas (deceased when recd)</td></tr>
</table>

<table>
<tr><td colspan="2">

Record of
Will West
Register No. 3426
</td></tr>
<tr><td>Sentenced</td><td>4-21-1903</td></tr>
<tr><td>Sentence</td><td>10 years & $50.00 Fine</td></tr>
<tr><td>Charge</td><td>Manslaughter</td></tr>
<tr><td>Court</td><td>WD-Indian Territory, Case #4 (Okmulgee, Okla)</td></tr>
<tr><td>Received</td><td>5-1-1903</td></tr>
<tr><td>Escaped</td><td>Discharged Expiration of Sentence 2-28-1909</td></tr>
<tr><td>Apprehended</td><td></td></tr>
<tr><td>Returned</td><td></td></tr>
<tr><td>Paroled</td><td></td></tr>
<tr><td>Pardoned</td><td></td></tr>
<tr><td>Born</td><td>Texas</td></tr>
<tr><td>Left home</td><td>Age 12</td></tr>
<tr><td>Education</td><td>Cannot read nor write</td></tr>
<tr><td>Occupation</td><td>Farmer</td></tr>
<tr><td>Religion</td><td>None</td></tr>
<tr><td>Usual Residence</td><td>Catoosa, I. T. (Okla)</td></tr>
<tr><td>Father Born</td><td>Texas</td></tr>
<tr><td>Mother Born</td><td>Texas (deceased when recd)</td></tr>
</table>

The fingerprints of government employees and applicants for federal jobs are included in the civil files. On an average day the FBI receives about 34,000 new fingerprint records.

The fingerprints are recorded on eight-inch square pieces of thin cardboard. The FBI has so many fingerprint records that if they were stacked in one pile, they would be as tall as New York's Empire State Building.

The FBI uses seven different fingerprint patterns to identify criminals: central pocket loop, double loop, accidental, plain arch, loop, plain whorl, and tented arch.

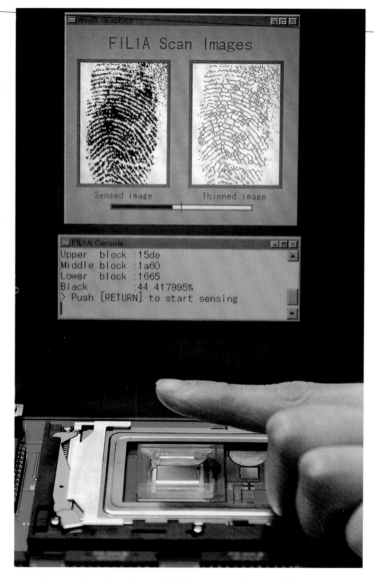

The FBI hopes that electronic fingerprint-checking technology, such as this system, developed by a company in Tokyo, Japan, will someday replace traditional fingerprint cards.

Central pocket loop: This pattern looks like the cross section of an onion, except that the concentric circles are often disconnected or broken.

Double loop: In this pattern, the concentric circles seem to swirl. The lines resemble the letter *S*.

Accidental: The main pattern resembles an extended, upside-down letter *U*.

Plain arch: This pattern is relatively level, compared to the other patterns. The lines are only slightly raised.

Loop: The main pattern resembles an elongated, upside-down letter *U.*

Plain whorl: This pattern most closely resembles a cross section of an onion or tree trunk. All of the concentric circles remain parallel. This is the most circular of all the patterns.

Tented Arch: This pattern resembles a tent and is triangular in shape.

The FBI is currently working on a fingerprint analysis system that will someday completely replace the traditional fingerprint card (and free up a lot of office space at the FBI Headquarters in Washington, D.C.). The new system, the Integrated Automated Fingerprint Identification System (IAFIS), will allow law enforcement officers to do electronic national fingerprint checks without using paper fingerprint cards.

When special agents investigate the scene of a crime, they carefully search for **latent fingerprints.** A latent fingerprint is any fingerprint left at a crime scene (as opposed to one on a fingerprint card). Humans leave latent fingerprints on almost all surfaces—glasses, doors, papers. They can even be left on human skin. Since these prints can be hard to see, the FBI uses several techniques designed to make the prints easier to detect and read. Agents may use lasers, powders, special lighting, or other techniques. Specially trained agents will then compare the prints to thousands of other prints in their database. They hope to find a match that will identify the criminal.

DNA Testing: A Different Kind of "Fingerprint"

To detect criminals, FBI agents may use a sophisticated identification method called **DNA** testing. Deoxyribonucleic acid, or DNA, is our individual "fingerprint" of living cells. The sequence, or order, of two strands of these cells shows a person's individual characteristics. DNA can be used much like fingerprinting to detect criminals or to link them to a crime.

To use this method, FBI agents must first extract the DNA from the evidence. If, for example, special agents find blood on the floor at the scene of a murder, they will collect a sample of the blood and send it to the lab for DNA testing. Law enforcement officers might also collect a blood sample from a suspect and send it to the lab for DNA testing. If the two sequences match, chances are good that the criminal has been identified.

It is usually not that easy, however. FBI agents often have to dig a bit deeper to solve mysteries. For example, a man was talking on a pay telephone. He told the person on the other end of the line that he had killed a woman and that

DNA from crime scene evidence is analyzed at the Florida Department of Law Enforcement's crime laboratory.

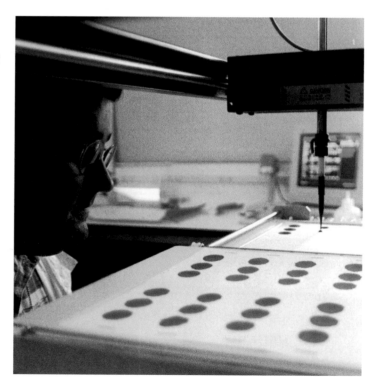

he had buried her body in the woods near a local park. Little did he know that a woman overheard his conversation. She quickly called the FBI.

The FBI, in turn, called the local police who found the woman's body. It had decomposed; just the skeleton remained. Since the officers could not identify the woman's body, they sent it to the FBI. Examiners extracted DNA from the woman's bones and performed a DNA analysis. After comparing it on a computer database that archived the DNA of missing people, examiners were able to identify the woman and eventually to catch and convict her killer, who was none other than the man on the phone.

In another case someone sent a threatening letter to a newspaper editor. The FBI lab recovered some saliva cells from the flap of the envelope and performed DNA testing on the sample. The agents compared the sample to a sample taken from a known suspect and found the man who had threatened the editor.

I Cannot Tell A Lie: Polygraph Testing

In ancient China if a person doubted whether another person was lying, the questioner gave the suspected liar a grain of rice to chew. If he could spit it out, he was innocent. If he could not produce enough saliva to spit out the grain of rice, he was lying. The ancient Chinese believed that guilt would absorb a person's saliva. In a sense they were right. Our bodies' physical reactions differ when we are lying and when we are telling the truth. The current polygraph machine is based on these ancient Chinese ideas.

In 1914 scientists began experimenting with lie detector machines. A pneumograph, for example, detected lies based on a person's breathing patterns. A galvanometer measured changes in the amount of perspiration on a person's fingertips. Unfortunately, however, these early methods were not very accurate.

John Larson and Leonard Keeler invented the modern lie detector test, the polygraph. This instrument was able to continually record changes in a person's blood pressure, pulse, breathing, and perspiration while the person answered questions. It is much the same test that FBI special agents and other law enforcement agents use today.

If the person being tested is lying, his body will react to that fear, and the detector will be able to measure those reactions.

A **polygraph test** is made up of three parts: the pretest interview, the test, and the post-test phase. Before beginning the first part, the examiner obtains information about the case from the investigator. Using this information, the examiner will write appropriate questions for the actual test. After creating the set of questions, the examiner is ready for the pretest interview.

In the pretest interview, the examiner will introduce himself or herself to the person being tested and will explain how the test works. The person being tested responds with his or her side of the story. Then the polygraph test begins.

The person being tested answers only yes or no to the series of questions. Through most of these questions, the examiner is trying to measure the individual's knowledge of, participation, or involvement in, the crime under investigation. The theory is that, during the polygraph test, the person being tested will react to the questions he or she finds most frightening. Often, the person being tested will lie about questions that scare him or her and will usually have a physical reaction to these questions. He or she might, for example, perspire more and breathe faster or his or her blood pressure might increase. These are all telltale signs of a lie.

To determine how a person will really respond when lying or telling the truth, the test will include questions that develop a standard—a sort of lie detector ruler—against which the examiner can measure. These standards are called truths and probable lies. A question to measure a probable truth for an eight-year-old male could be, "Are you eight years old?" to which the person being tested would truthfully respond "Yes." The probable-lie question might be, "Have you ever lied to someone who trusted you?" The examiner records the blood pressure, pulse, perspiration, and respiration of the person being tested during both questions and then compares those results to the results recorded for actual questions regarding the crime.

After the examiner finishes asking the questions, he or she will study the results to determine if the person being tested lied or told the truth. If the polygraph shows the person was telling the truth, the person is free to leave. If it shows the person was lying, the person must answer more questions. In this phase the examiner tries to convince the person being tested to tell the truth. The examiner tries to make the person being tested feel more comfortable and tries to ask pointed questions.

Besides identifying lies, a polygraph can also rule out suspects and verify witnesses' statements or informant information about a crime. Polygraph tests are fairly accurate.

The Fine Art of Catching Crooks

When FBI agents or the police are looking for a criminal, they often ask an artist to draw a picture, based on a physical description a witness provides. Sometimes a computer generates these drawings, but usually an artist draws the portrait by hand.

The artist must listen very carefully to the witness's description and must ask the witness leading questions that might narrow down the features and characteristics of the person. On average, it takes an artist about two or three hours to draw a picture, or composite.

One of the most successful results of an artist's composite was in the case of the bombing of the Federal Building in Oklahoma City in 1995. Drawings of the suspects were displayed on television and in newspapers. When one man was captured a few days after the bombing, his appearance was uncannily similar to the man the artist had sketched.

When a case has been open for a long time, catching the criminal by means of an old photo may be difficult. He might, for example, have lost his hair, put on weight, or obtained glasses. FBI specialists can age-enhance a photo, based on the probability of what that person will look like in a certain number of years.

A Dog's Life: Some Special FBI "Members"

Because of their superior sense of smell and their intelligence, there are some jobs—like detecting explosives and narcotics and finding people in distress—that our canine friends can do better than humans. Just like their human counterparts, these special FBI "agents" undergo many hours of rigorous training to earn their titles.

By instinct, dogs know how to find things. A handler, the dog's human partner, teaches the dog what to look for. A dog might use its senses of hearing, seeing, and smelling to find what it's looking for.

The dog's handler is generally an FBI special agent, and the two work together as a team. The handler trains the dog to find very specific things, such as a bomb, a person, or drugs in unusual places—for example, deep in the woods, buried in a hole in the ground, or locked in a suitcase.

Dogs often live with their handlers. They may become best friends as well as teammates. Besides sniffing out evidence and locating missing people, these canines also earn their bones by giving demonstrations in schools and other organizations.

Search and Rescue Dogs

When a disaster such as an earthquake or a tornado hits or a crime occurs, FBI agents enlist the help of search and rescue dogs, or S and Rs. These canines rescue people who are trapped or missing. They often locate missing children.

In the case of a crime, these dogs can smell an article of the suspect's clothing, and "sniff out" clues that help agents capture the criminal. The S and Rs have such an excellent sense of smell that they can almost always find what they are looking for, even if it is underground or underwater.

Chemical Explosion Dogs

Chemical explosion dogs learn at an early age how to seek out various explosive chemicals. Handlers also teach these dogs not to get too excited when they do detect something explosive, as jumping up and down on a bomb might cause it to explode. The dogs let their handlers know they have found something by sitting down quietly in the area where they smell the substance. These dogs are also used to sniff out possible explosives at large events such as football games or concerts.

Narcotics Detection Dogs

Even though humans could probably not detect the difference, each drug has its own smell, and narcotics detection dogs learn to identify several different drugs by scent. When a dog smells a drug, it scratches the area; the handler then retrieves the illegal substance.

A dog trained to smell out fire-starting liquids assists FBI officials in an investigation of three synagogue fires.

The FBI Laboratory

FBI scientists are the people behind the prosecution of many federal crimes. Through their careful analysis of evidence, these scientists have helped bring many criminals to justice. Likewise, thanks to their efforts, many innocent people are not wrongly prosecuted.

The FBI laboratory is one of the biggest and best-equipped forensic laboratories in the world. The laboratory's scientists examine evidence free of charge for federal, state, and local law enforcement agencies. They also give expert witness testimony in court regarding the results of their examinations.

The laboratory has been housed in the new J. Edgar Hoover building in Washington, D.C., since 1974. The public can take a tour of the laboratory, but the tour route is separated from the actual laboratory work space. The laboratory's Forensic Science Research and Training Center opened at the FBI Academy in Quantico, Virginia, in 1981.

The FBI receives so much general mail each day that the headquarters building in Washington, D.C., actually has its own zip code: 20535. Each day the laboratory might receive 600 pieces of evidence to examine, ranging in size from a tiny drop of blood to a chunk of wall with a bullet hole.

It takes a lot of money and people to run the FBI. The FBI's budget for fiscal year 1999, for example, was $3.1 billion. As of October 1, 1998, about 11,400 special agents and 16,400 professional support personnel worked for the FBI. Each of these FBI employees strives to live up to the FBI motto—fidelity, bravery, integrity. Thanks to the work of these people, America is undoubtedly a safer place.

Glossary

Counterintelligence—Organized activity designed to block an enemy's sources of information, to deceive the enemy, to prevent sabotage, or to gather information.

DNA—Deoxyribonucleic acid, a chemical blueprint that identifies individual human beings.

Fingerprinting—A crime detection technique, invented in the early 1900s, which identifies a criminal by the marks left on an object by the unique ridges and swirls on his hands and fingers.

Intelligence—Obtaining secret information.

JD—Juris doctorate, latin for doctor of law. A law degree.

Latent fingerprint—Any fingerprint left at a crime scene (as opposed to on a fingerprint card).

Polygraph testing—A test given to determine if a person is lying.

Rookie—A special agent trainee.

Sabotage—The destruction of property in order to stop a cause or endeavor.

Surveillance—The observation of a person, place, or thing by a person or a camera.

Terrorism—When a group uses violence and intimidation to achieve a goal or send a message.

Further Reading

Books

D'Angelo, Laura. *The FBI's Most Wanted.* Philadelphia: Chelsea House, 1997.

Diarmuid, Jeffreys. *The Bureau: Inside the Modern FBI.* New York: Houghton Mifflin, 1995.

Fisher, David. *Hard Evidence: How Detectives Inside the FBI's Sci-Crime Lab Have Helped Solve America's Toughest Cases.* New York: Simon & Schuster, 1995.

Jones, Charlotte Foltz. *Fingerprints and Talking Bones: How Real-Life Crimes are Solved.* New York: Delacorte, 1997.

Kelly, John F. and Phillip K. Wearne. *Tainting Evidence: Inside the Scandals at the FBI Crime Lab.* New York: The Free Press, 1998.

Websites

University of San Diego
http://ac.acusd.edu/History/classes/20th/FBI.html

FBI website
www.fbi.gov (1999)

Index

ABOUT THE AUTHOR: Dynise Balcavage is a writer and graphic designer who lives in Philadelphia. She has written three other books, *Ludwig van Beethoven, Steroids,* and *The Great Chicago Fire,* as well as many magazine articles.

SENIOR CONSULTING EDITOR Arthur M. Schlesinger, jr. is the leading American historian of our time. He won the Pulitzer Prize for his book *The Age of Jackson* (1945) and again for *A Thousand Days* (1965). This chronicle of the Kennedy Administration also won a National Book Award. Professor Schlesinger is the Albert Schweitzer Professor of the Humanities at the City University of New York, and has been involved in several other Chelsea House projects, including the REVOLUTIONARY WAR LEADERS and COLONIAL LEADERS series.